CU00920695

Fermented Fooas vol. 2: Milk Kefir

Written by Meghan Grande

This book contains material protected under International and Federal Copyright Laws and Treaties. Any unauthorized reprint or use of this material is prohibited. No part of this book may be reproduced or transmitted in any form or by any means, electronic or mechanical, including photocopying, recording, or by any information storage and retrieval system without express written permission from the author.

© 2014 All rights reserved.

Book 2 of **The Food Preservation Series** of Books

Disclaimer:

The information contained in this book is for general information purposes only.

While we endeavor to keep the information up to date and correct, we make no representations or warranties of any kind, express or implied, about the completeness, accuracy, reliability, suitability or availability with respect to the book or the information, products, services, or related graphics contained in the book for any purpose. Any reliance you place on such information is therefore strictly at your own risk.

None of the information in this this book is meant to be construed as medical advice. Always consult with a medical profession prior to making any dietary changes in your life.

This book is about fermented milk products. The author of the book is not a trained professional in food safety or any related field. Neither the author nor the publisher is responsible for any damages arising from the use or misuse of the information provided in this book.

Contents

Introduction

The first book in this series, *Fermented Foods vol. 1: Fermented Vegetables*, was written on a topic most people are familiar with. Next to yogurt, fermented vegetables rank amongst the most popular fermented foods in existence. You'd be hard-pressed to find someone who hasn't heard of sauerkraut and most people will tell you they've at least sampled it once or twice.

The second book in the series, on the other hand, is about a fermented milk product that's just now starting to grow in popularity in the Western world. Most people's knowledge of fermented milk products extends as far as the realm of yogurt and maybe buttermilk. If you can name more fermented milk products than just those two, consider yourself well-informed. Mention milk kefir and kefir grains to the average person and you'll more than likely be met with a blank stare. It's too bad, really, because unlike yogurt, kefir doesn't require a strictly temperature-controlled environment and is much easier to make. It's loaded with nutrients, has more probiotic bacteria than yogurt and arguably tastes better than its more-popular cousin.

The story of milk kefir and the famed kefir grains used to create it is steeped in legend. It's been rumored the original milk kefir grains were a gift from the prophet Mohammed, handed down to nomadic shepherds in the Caucuses Mountains that run from the Caspian Sea to the Black Sea, separating Georgia from Russia. The original grains were known as "The Grains of the Prophet" and were kept a secret for many years by the tribes of shepherds who held them (1).

Like all good secrets, the secret of the magical grains eventually found its way out of the mountains and spread throughout Russia and the rest of the world. While milk kefir is relatively unknown in the Western world, it's the most popular fermented beverage in Russia and can be found pretty much anywhere Eastern Europeans have immigrated.

What Is Milk Kefir?

The word *kefir* is derived from the Turkish word "keyif," which means "feeling good" when translated to English. This is likely due to the fact that people who consume kefir often claim to be in good health and live long lives.

Milk kefir is a fermented milk product made by placing kefir grains into milk and allowing the bacteria and yeasts in the grains to ferment the milk. It can be made from the milk of pretty much any animal you'd want to drink the milk of. Cow, goat and sheep milk can all be used as a base for milk kefir. Coconut milk and soy milk can also be used, as long as you occasionally return your grains to animal milk so they can recharge.

Milk kefir is made from *milk kefir grains*, which are a symbiotic colony of lactobacteria and yeast. If you're familiar with vegetable ferments, you'll recognize lactobacteria as being the same bacteria responsible for fermenting vegetables. Milk kefir grains most closely resemble small cauliflower curds in look and they feel soft and pliable to the touch. A tablespoon or two of grains is usually all that's needed to get a ferment off and running.

Milk kefir isn't as thick as yogurt and can be poured out of the container. It falls somewhere between yogurt and milk as far as consistency is concerned. It has a lightly tangy taste and a light, effervescent mouthfeel to it. The tangy aftertaste requires a little getting used to, but you'll soon find yourself craving this tasty beverage, especially once you've learned to flavor it with fresh fruit and a number of other ingredients.

I've heard milk kefir described as being a "sparkling yogurt," and that's a fairly accurate description of the way it tastes. The similarities end there, however, as milk kefir rises above and beyond yogurt when it comes to nutritional value and it contains a more robust probiotic profile. I won't go so far as to say you should stop eating yogurt if you like it, but I will say most people could easily replace yogurt with kefir without skipping a beat. This is especially true if the yogurt you're eating come from the refrigerated foods section of your local grocery store.

Nutrients in Milk Kefir

For many years, the grains used to ferment milk kefir were believed to have magical powers. That's as good of an explanation as any, as scientists still haven't unlocked many of the secrets of kefir and its grains. While very little is known about kefir, scientists have managed to determine it's good for most people.

A single serving of milk kefir is relatively low in calories, ranging from 60 to 120 calories per serving, depending on what has been added to the kefir and what type of milk was used. Milk kefir is also low-fat, as it only contains around 4 grams of fat per serving. You get nearly 10 grams of natural protein, 20% of your daily recommended value of calcium and a number of other vitamins and minerals as part of the package as well.

Here are just some of the many nutrients found in milk kefir:

- **Amino acids.**
- **Calcium.**
- **Carotene.**
- **Chloride.**
- **Copper.**
- **Folic acid.**
- **Iron.**
- **Kefiran.**
- **Magnesium.**
- **Magnesium.**
- **Molybdenum.**

- Niacin.
- Phosphor.
- Potassium.
- Protein.
- Thiamin.
- Vitamin A.
- Vitamin C.
- Vitamin D.
- Vitamin E.
- Vitamins B2, B6 and B12.
- Vitamin K2.
- Zinc.

The proteins in kefir are *predigested*, meaning they're partially broken down during fermentation. This makes proteins that are difficult to digest more accessible to the body. The casein protein found in milk can be difficult for people to digest and may cause gastrointestinal distress. People who have difficulty digesting casein may be able to tolerate milk kefir due to the predigestion that takes place during fermentation. What this means is your body may be able to take up more protein from milk kefir than it would if you drank a similar-sized serving of milk.

All-in-all, milk kefir packs a strong nutritional punch. It's no wonder it keeps showing up near the top of lists of superfoods. There isn't a whole lot not to like about milk kefir.

The Health Benefits of Milk Kefir

Milk kefir has been widely researched in Russia, but much of that research hasn't been translated and isn't easily accessible. Scientists in the Western world are just starting to unlock the many health benefits of milk kefir and what they've found thus far has largely been promising.

One odd feature of milk kefir is even though it's full of probiotic bacteria, it has strong antibiotic properties. It's been shown to enhance triple therapy treatment in patients infected with *Helicobacter pylori* while reducing side effects (2). Antimicrobial activity has also been recorded against *candida albicans, salmonella typhi, staphylococcus aureus* and *E. coli* (3). This is likely due to a number of factors. The lactic acid in milk kefir creates an environment that allows beneficial bacteria to grow but hinders the growth of harmful bacteria.

Additionally, adding large numbers of probiotic bacteria to the gut helps crowd out harmful bacteria. Think of the gut as a subway station. The bad bacteria are robbers creeping through the station, looking for victims and the good bacteria are little police officers who keep the robbers away from their victims. When the robbers outnumber the police, things can get bad in a hurry. Eating probiotic foods introduces large numbers of police to the station and tilts things in the favor of the good guys.

In addition to keeping the gut in good health, probiotic bacteria play a number of roles in the body.

The friendly bacteria in kefir have been shown in a laboratory setting to block a specific antibody responsible for certain allergies. Since it reduces the levels of the antibody over time, long-term consumption of milk kefir may help dampen allergic response (4).

A Chinese study published in 2013 by Jilin University in China reveals that three of the strains of lactobacteria found in milk kefir lower bad cholesterol and two of the strains raise good cholesterol in testing done on lab rats (5). Studies done on humans have shown conflicting results, but at least one Japanese study has shown fermented milk supplemented with whey protein to have a positive effect on both cholesterol and systolic blood pressure (6).

People who are lactose intolerant and aren't able to handle most dairy products may be able to tolerate milk kefir. In a small study of adults suffering from lactose maldigestion, kefir was shown to reduce flatulence, abdominal pain and diarrhea symptoms (7). While kefir may not work for everyone, this study on kefir and a handful of studies on probiotic yogurt have shown promising results.

Another area in which milk kefir has shown promising results is in cancer research. The effect of kefir on tumors in humans hasn't been studied, but there are a number of studies of the effect of kefir on tumors in animals. One such study on sarcoma tumor cells in mice found that milk kefir inhibited tumor growth by 64.8%,while soy milk kefir inhibited growth by 70.9%. This led researchers to conclude "milk and soy kefirs may be considered among the more promising food components in terms of cancer prevention" (8). Another study found that a kefir product containing a specific strain of lactobacteria known as *lactobacillus kefiri* had the ability to punch holes in multi-drug resistant myeloid leukemia cells (9).

Bacteria in Your Body

Most people are brought up believing all bacteria are bad. We're taught from an early age that bacteria are the reason we get sick and great pains are taken to avoid bacteria at all costs. We use antibacterial soaps to wash our hands. We clean our counters with antibacterial wipes. We take antibiotics to kill bacteria in our bodies that are making us ill. To top things off, aside from yogurt, the vast majority of foods we eat have been sterilized to remove any and all bacteria that may have once resided in the food.

We live in a largely sterile world and use a number of products to help ensure it stays that way. Turn back the clock a short ways to the beginning of the previous century and our lives were teeming with bacteria. We ate them, we had them on our hands and bodies and we lived in homes that were full of them. And you know what? We got along just fine. In fact, the argument could be made that we were healthier then than we are now. Cancer, heart disease and obesity rates were much lower then than they are now.

Intentionally eating bacteria in food seems like such a foreign concept to some people that they absolutely refuse to believe the probiotic bacteria in fermented foods are actually good for the human body. According to these people, if it's labeled as bacteria, it's automatically evil in their book.

The funny thing is you're never going to get away from bacteria. Trillions upon trillions of bacteria have taken up residence in your body and have no plans on going anywhere anytime soon. In fact, your body houses 10 times the number of bacteria than it does cells. There are somewhere in the neighborhood of 10 trillion cells in the body, which sounds like a lot until you realize there are 100 trillion bacteria (10). That's right…You're made up of more bacteria than you are the building blocks of life.

Before you run to the store looking for a product that'll cleanse all of the bacteria from your body, take a deep breath and relax. They're supposed to be there and they benefit the body in a number of ways. One area in the body where vast numbers of bacteria congregate is your digestive system, collectively referred to as **the gut**. Bacteria in the gut are responsible for boosting the immune system, helping nourish the brain and fighting off harmful bacteria that already exist in the gut or are introduced to the gut in the foods we eat (11).

A number of problems can arise when the gut is unhealthy and one of the keys to ensuring good gut health is to properly maintain the levels of beneficial bacteria that take up residence there. When the numbers of beneficial bacteria drop too low, all sorts of problems can arise, ranging from mild problems like gastrointestinal distress and diarrhea to more severe health issues like autoimmune disorders and cancers. Poor gut health is believed to be a contributing factor to a number of diseases and ailments and allowing your gut to spiral out of control can result in symptoms arising all over the body.

Bacteria in Milk Kefir

Consumption of probiotic foods is one way to help ensure the gut maintains healthy levels of beneficial bacteria. A single serving of a probiotic food can add billions or even trillions of beneficial bacteria to the gut.

Milk kefir is one of the most highly-probiotic foods known to man. A small bowl of milk kefir reportedly contains up to 5 trillion bacterial cultures. That's significantly more cultures than are found in a similar-sized bowl of yogurt, which has somewhere around 1.5 trillion microorganisms and way more than your average probiotic supplement capsule, which contains around 15 billion bacteria (12).

The exact number and type of bacteria found in any given ferment largely depends on the kefir grains that are used and the environment in which fermentation takes place. If you took kefir grains from Russia and fermented milk with them, the resultant kefir would have a different probiotic profile than milk kefir made from grains sourced in the United States. Similarly, if you took grains from a single location and divided them up and made milk kefir in two different places in the world, you'd end up with different probiotic profiles in each of the ferments.

The total number of different strains and varieties bacteria and yeasts found in kefir could be a couple hundred or more. Here are just some of the many bacteria and yeasts known to exist in milk kefir:

- *Candida humilis*
- *Kazachstania exigua*

- *Kazachstania unispora*
- *Kluyveromyces lactis*
- *Kluyveromyces marxianus*
- *Kluyveromyces siamensis*
- *Lactobacillus acidophilus*
- *Lactobacillus brevis*
- *Lactobacillus casei*
- *Lactobacillus delbrueckii*
- *Lactobacillus fermentum*
- *Lactobacillus helveticus*
- *Lactobacillus kefiranofaciens*
- *Lactobacillus kefiri*
- *Lactobacillus paracasei*
- *Lactobacillus parakefiri.*
- *Lactobacillus plantarum*
- *Lactobacillus rhamnosus*
- *Lactobacillus sake*
- *Lactococcus lactis*
- *Lactococcus lactis*
- *Leuconostoc mesenteroides*
- *Pseudomonas fluorescens*
- *Pseudomonas putida*
- *Saccharomyces cerevisiae*
- *Saccharomyces martiniae*
- *Saccharomyces unisporus*
- *Streptococcus thermophilus*

In addition to the bacteria and yeasts listed, a number of other bacteria and yeasts may reside in milk kefir. Additionally, there are a number of subspecies of the listed bacteria and yeast types that may make an appearance in a kefir ferment. Kefir ferments are known as *wild ferments* because the fermenter has little control over the exact types of bacteria that end up in the final product.

The Milk Kefir Grain

Kefir grains range in size from tiny specks to a few inches in diameter or larger and have a bumpy, irregular surface that at first glance is reminiscent of cauliflower florets. The resemblance stops there, however, as they're pliable and elastic to the touch. They're usually white or pale yellow in color and have rich, yeasty smell.

The composition of milk kefir grains is difficult to describe because so little is known about what is actually going on inside the grain. What is known is kefir grains are made up of a symbiotic colony of bacteria and yeasts that thrive when placed into milk and left to work their magic. Each colony of grains is different from other colonies and can differ from grain to grain in the same colony. The typical milk kefir grain has a microbial composition of around 90% lactobacteria and 10% yeasts, with a small amount acetic acid bacteria and other organisms thrown in for good measure. The portion of the grain you can see is mixture of complex sugars, amino acids, lipids and insoluble protein (13).

Kefir grains are largely a product of their environment and will pull bacteria out of the air and from surrounding ferments. Kefir grains can be contaminated by molds and other organisms capable of floating through the air.

When placed into milk, kefir grains can replicate and begin to grow. The rate of growth varies from colony to colony, with some growing at a snail's pace, while others seemingly double in size every couple of days. The rate at which kefir grains are able to ferment milk also varies. Some colonies of grains act quickly and can ferment milk overnight, while others chug along slowly and require extra time to get the job done.

When properly cared for and fed, kefir grains can last for years and can be used to ferment batch after batch of kefir. I rarely run into others who ferment kefir, but the few I have come across are usually willing to share their grains if they have any extras. If you're lucky enough to find someone willing to part with enough grains for you to start your own kefir ferment, consider yourself very lucky. If not, there's always the Internet. All you're going to need is a tablespoon or two of grains and before you know it, you'll have more than you know what to do with.

What Happens During a Ferment?

Milk kefir grains need milk to survive. When properly dried and stored, they can last a long time without it, but the grains will eventually lose effectiveness and may die off.

When placed into a container of milk, the lactobacteria in the grains are the first to go to work and they start processing the lactose in the milk almost immediately. As they process the lactose, lactic acid is created as a byproduct. The yeasts in the kefir grains slowly wake up and begin processing lactose and proteins in the milk, consuming oxygen and creating CO_2 and small amounts of ethanol. By the time fermentation is complete, there is very little lactose left in milk. This is the reason people who are lactose intolerant are often able to tolerate milk kefir.

Once fermentation has taken place, the following compounds are known to exist in kefir:

- **Acetic acid bacteria.**
- **Carbon dioxide.**
- **Ethanol.**
- **Kefiran.**
- **Lactic acid bacteria.**
- **Milk proteins.**
- **Polysaccharides.**
- **Vitamins and minerals.**
- **Water.**
- **Yeasts.**

The exact breakdown of the compounds found in a batch of kefir varies, as fermentation is a highly-dynamic process. The original composition of the kefir grains, the amount of grains used, the type of milk used and a number of environmental factors all affect the composition of the final product. You can safely assume there is a variety of beneficial microflora in the kefir, but there's no way of telling exactly what's in a ferment without laboratory testing.

You may have noticed ethanol is a byproduct of fermentation. While it's true there's a small amount of alcohol created during fermentation, it's rarely enough to be of concern. One thing to keep in mind is the longer you ferment milk kefir, the more alcohol it's going to contain. Even then it usually isn't enough to worry about. Even the longer ferments rarely contain more than 1% alcohol by volume.

What's Better? Buying Kefir or Making It Yourself?

As kefir grows in popularity, it's showing up in places where I never thought I'd see it. I've seen milk kefir in health food stores, which is to be expected, but I've also recently seen it sitting with the yogurt in both grocery stores and convenience stores. My experience with store-bought milk kefir is admittedly thin, but I prefer homemade kefir for a number of reasons.

For one, the varieties of kefir you can purchase in the store are lacking in comparison to the varieties you can make at home. There are a vast number of ingredients that can be added to homemade kefir to naturally flavor and sweeten it and you have ultimate control over what goes into your kefir if you're the person making it. Commercial kefir has additives added to keep it fresh and chemicals may leach into the kefir from the plastic container it's stored in.

While commercial kefir does contain bacterial cultures, it typically isn't made in the same manner you'd make kefir at home and doesn't contain all of the bacteria and yeasts home-fermented kefir has. Some companies create blends of probiotic bacteria that are similar to what you'd find in kefir and use them to ferment their kefir. Others use a central batch of kefir that uses milk kefir grains, but when they're making individual batches for sale, they pull kefir from the mother batch and use it to ferment the milk instead of using the grains. Both of these techniques are attempts by the company making the kefir to standardize the flavor and the ingredients that go into their kefir, so customers get the same thing every time they buy their product.

As you'll soon find out, home ferments rarely taste the same from batch to batch and often seemingly have a mind of their own. This can be frustrating, as you never know exactly what you're going to end up with, but it's a good trait when you have a batch or two you don't particularly care for. You know that at some point it's going to change anyway, so you don't have to throw out your grains and start over.

Another problem with commercial kefir is it has had the yeast fermentation process halted, so the kefir doesn't continue to ferment in the bottle. This is likely because stores would be reluctant to carry kefir that popped its top when it sat on the shelf for too long. This second fermentation is the reason why homemade kefir has a slight fizz to it. If you like your kefir lightly carbonated, you aren't going to get that from commercial kefir.

Some stores are beginning to sell kefir packets that can be used to ferment a single batch of kefir. These packets are often single-use packets and you have to use a new one every time you want to make a batch of kefir. Some packets are designed to where you can use kefir from previous ferments to make future batches of kefir, but each batch gets progressively weaker over time. Kefir made in this manner contains fewer strains of probiotic bacteria than a traditional kefir ferment does and they don't offer the same health benefits as regular kefir.

In addition to getting more probiotic bacteria and less chemicals, you'll also save some cash by making your own milk kefir at home. A bottle of kefir bought from a grocery store will run you upwards of $4.00 for 32 ounces. If you drink a bottle a week, which is an extremely low estimate in my household, you'll spend $208. If you buy kefir grains and reuse them to ferment milk you've purchased from the store, you'll end up spending half that for the same amount of kefir.

If you don't have time or the desire to make your own kefir, you can buy kefir from the store and get some, but not all, of the benefits you'd get if you made it yourself. It really isn't all that much work to make your own kefir and you'll be able to rest easy knowing you're getting the full health value from your homemade probiotic beverage. Milk

The Fermenting Jar

Milk kefir was traditionally made in bags made of sheepskin or goatskin. The bag was left hanging in the sun all day and as darkness fell, the bag was brought in and hung by the door and everyone gave it a shake as they came into the house (1). Luckily, kefir doesn't have to be made this way, or I suspect it wouldn't be as popular as it is now. I can't think of too many people who would want an animal skin sack full of milk hanging by the front door.

The type of vessel you use for fermenting kefir is up to you. As long as it's made from a non-reactive material like ceramic, porcelain or glass and can be covered to keep insects out, you have free reign to choose the container that best suits your needs. Some people use plastic containers, but I worry about chemicals leaching from the plastic into my kefir.

If you decide to use ceramic, make sure it's safe for use and doesn't contain lead. A lot of the older ceramic jars (and even some of the newer ones) have lead in the glaze that can leach into foods that are stored in the jar. If you aren't sure, it's best to find another jar. You're eating kefir to feel better, not to get lead poisoning! Make sure your container is safe to use.

I like to keep it simple and prefer glass canning jars, either of the one-quart or the half-gallon variety. I've also used tall carafes, but have found they're a bit difficult to cover. Canning jars are inexpensive, made of glass, which is as non-reactive as it gets and are easy to cover. Another nice thing about canning jars is you can store the kefir in the same container you made it in. All you need to do is filter out the grains, put an airtight lid on it and move it to the fridge.

There are more expensive jars on the market made just for fermenting kefir, but there's really no reason to spend a lot of money on them unless you really want a dedicated fermenting container.

Kefir Safety

While most experts on milk kefir consider it relatively safe, there are occasionally times when something will go wrong during a ferment and the milk will go bad instead of properly fermenting. There will usually be signs the kefir has gone bad, so pay close attention to what's going on in the jar.

It's rare, but mold may start to grow on the surface of the kefir in a container. This is more common in longer ferments than shorter ones. If you open a jar and find mold growing, throw out both the kefir and the grains. Sterilize the jar before using it again, as small spores may be left behind when you dump out the kefir.

Insects and animals love kefir. Keep it out of reach of animals that roam around the house. Insects can be more problematic, as they can seemingly find food anywhere you put it. It's important to make sure you properly cover the container. Kefir ferments are done using a container into which air is allowed to flow freely, but care should be taken to keep insects out. Cover the jar with a light towel or a few pieces of cheesecloth and secure it in place tightly with a rubber band or a piece of twine tied around the neck of the jar. If there is any indication insects have invaded your kefir, get rid of both the kefir and the grains because the insects may have laid eggs in the kefir. Sterilize the jar before use.

When it's all said and done, your senses of sight, taste and smell are your best defense regarding kefir that may have turned instead of fermenting. If it looks, smells or tastes bad, don't consume it. Toss both the kefir and the grains and start over again from scratch. The stakes are too high to play around with potentially-spoiled milk.

Storing Milk Kefir

Milk kefir will last up to a month stored in the fridge. Once you've fermented the kefir, place it into an airtight container and store the container in the coldest part of your refrigerator.

The cold will slow the bacteria and yeasts to a crawl. They'll still continue to ferment the kefir, but it'll be at a much slower rate of speed than it would be if you left the kefir on the counter. You may be able to get away with storing kefir for a longer period of time, but I've found it gets too sour and too much carbonation builds up in it. Properly-fermented kefir doesn't go bad inasmuch as it gets too sour and acidic to drink.

Kefir should be stored in an airtight container. If storing kefir for more than a few days, open the container periodically to allow it to off-gas. If not, you could end up with a big mess in your refrigerator if too much pressure builds up.

For longer-term storage, milk kefir can be frozen. Freezing will make the bacteria in the kefir go dormant and will stop fermentation dead in its tracks, but won't kill them off unless the kefir is left in the freezer for too long. I rarely freeze kefir, but when I do, I try to use it within a couple months. Once you thaw it out, the probiotic bacteria should wake right back up.

Getting Started: Recharging the Grains

OK. You order your grains and they arrive a few days later. You open the package and find the grains have been preserved for shipping. Some suppliers freeze-dry their grains, while others send them in a small container of milk that may or may not still be providing sustenance to the grains. No matter how the grains are sent, there's a pretty good chance you're going to need to rehydrate and/or recharge them before they're able to produce good kefir.

In order to get your grains ready for use, you're going to need the following items:

- **A glass jar.**
- **A thin towel or some other breathable object you can use as a cover.**
- **A large rubber band or some twine.**
- **A large wood or plastic spoon.**
- **A plastic or stainless steel mesh strainer.**
- **Kefir grains.**
- **Fresh milk.**

Notice the lack of metal (other than the stainless steel strainer, if that's the type you go with). Metals like aluminum, tin and copper are reactive and may react with the acids in the kefir. They may also contaminate the grains and change the way they taste. If you go with the stainless steel strainer, make sure it's actually made of stainless steel before you use it. You don't want to ruin your kefir grains.

The type of milk you use doesn't matter, but don't buy it and leave it sitting in your fridge until right before it expires. Use as fresh of milk as possible.

Follow these directions to prepare the kefir grains for use:

1. Wash the glass jar, the spoon and the strainer. Don't use bleach or antibacterial soap and make sure you rinse out any soap you do use. Wash your hands as well, in order to avoid introducing bacteria to the grains.
2. Place the kefir grains into the jar. For each tablespoon of grains you have, add one cup of milk to the jar. Stir the milk and grains up a bit.
3. Cover the jar with the towel and secure it in place with the rubber band or some twine. Let it sit at room temperature for 24 hours. The ideal ambient temperature in the area where fermentation is done is around 75° F, but it can take place at hotter or cooler temperatures. If the temperature is cooler, it'll take longer for the milk to ferment. If it's warmer, fermentation will take place faster, as long as the temperature isn't hot enough to kill the bacteria. Make sure the container isn't in direct sunlight and move it to a cool cabinet or root cellar if you're concerned it might get too hot.
4. After 24 hours have passed, strain the kefir grains out of the milk. Discard the milk and return the kefir grains to the jar. Add fresh milk to the jar and cover it again.

5. Repeat this process for 1 to 2 weeks. Each successive day that passes, the milk should smell sourer and thicken up a bit more. Once the milk is consistently coagulating during fermentation, you're in business. The grains should start making consistently good kefir within the first couple weeks of use.

Milk kefir grains can occasionally be stubborn and may take up to a month to start consistently producing good kefir. After a couple weeks have passed without any results, try a longer 48-hour ferment or two to see if it helps. If you simply can't get the grains to work, contact the supplier and ask them to replace the grains.

Getting Started: Plain Kefir

If you had to recharge your grains, you've pretty much gone through the fermentation process over and over until the grains were producing good kefir. The only difference is this time you're fermenting it so you can drink it.

You're going to need the exact same supplies you used to recharge the grains. To recap, here are the supplies you'll need:

- **A glass jar.**
- **A thin towel or some other breathable object you can use as a cover.**
- **A large rubber band or some twine.**
- **A large wood or plastic spoon.**
- **A plastic or stainless steel mesh strainer.**
- **Kefir grains.**
- **Fresh milk.**

Now that your kefir grains are chugging along at full speed, you no longer need a cup of milk for every tablespoon of grains. This time around, all you need is one to three tablespoons of grains to ferment an entire quart of milk. If you don't have a tablespoon of grains, you can either try fermenting a quart of milk with the grains you do have or you can ferment smaller quantities of milk until your grains have had a chance to grow. You'll have to play around with the amount of grains you use until you determine the correct amount. Some grains work fast and are capable of fermenting large amounts of kefir with a small amount of grains, while others move slowly and you'll need more grains to ferment the same amount of milk.

Here are the directions for fermenting a batch of milk kefir:

1. Start with clean hands and a clean jar and utensils.
2. Add the kefir grains to the jar.
3. Add a quart of milk to the jar.
4. Gently stir the contents of the jar.
5. Cover the jar with cheesecloth or a thin towel and secure it in place.
6. Set the jar out to ferment at room temperature. Leave it to ferment for 18 to 24 hours.
7. Once the kefir has fermented, strain the grains out of the milk kefir. Move the grains to a new jar of milk. Seal the jar you just finished fermenting and move it to the fridge.

Practice this plain kefir recipe until you get it right. It's the basis for the rest of the recipes in the book. If you're having trouble making plain kefir, take the time to perfect it before moving on to the other recipes.

Build On It: Fizzy Kefir

Fizzy kefir isn't quite as sour as plain milk kefir. It's naturally carbonated and has an effervescent mouthfeel. There are people who love to drink it like this, but to me it's always tasted like carbonated plain yogurt. You can drink it plain if you like it that way, but this recipe really doesn't come into its own until you start adding natural flavors to it.

If you've taken the time to master the art of making plain kefir, this recipe is really easy. Once you've made plain milk kefir, you put the kefir you've made through a process known as a *second ferment*. This ferment gives the yeasts in the kefir time to go to work and adds carbonation in the form of CO_2 to the kefir. It also adds more probiotics to the kefir, along with additional vitamins and nutrients.

Here are the directions you need to follow in order to make fizzy kefir:

1. Make plain kefir. Strain the grains out and transfer them to a new jar of milk. The second ferment is done without the kefir grains being present in the jar.
2. Take the plain kefir and place it in a jar that can be sealed.
3. Seal the jar.
4. Leave the kefir to ferment at room temperature for an addition 12 to 24 hours. The longer you leave it to ferment, the more carbonation it'll have. It'll also have more alcohol content, so that's something to take into consideration.

5. Once the kefir is carbonated to your preference, move it to the fridge. It's a good idea to open the container to release any gases that have built up before moving it to cold storage.

You've now got fizzy kefir, which opens up a whole new world of possibilities. The recipes in this book will call for either plain milk kefir or fizzy milk kefir. Plain milk kefir gets a single ferment, while fizzy milk kefir undergoes a second ferment.

Kefir Sour Cream

Kefir sour cream is almost as easy to make as plain kefir. You add cream to the jar instead of regular milk and let it ferment just like you would regular kefir. The only difference comes when it's time to strain out your grains. It's a lot harder separating kefir grains from kefir sour cream because of its thick consistency.

I've found kefir sour cream can be used in most recipes that call for regular sour cream. It's somewhat of a waste to use it in recipes that call for cooking the sour cream because the probiotic bacteria are killed by the heat.

Ingredients:

1 quart milk cream.
2 tablespoons kefir grains.

Directions:

1. Start with clean hands and a clean jar and utensils.
2. Add the kefir grains to the jar.
3. Add a quart of milk cream to the jar.
4. Gently stir the cream.
5. Cover the jar with cheesecloth or a thin towel and secure it in place.
6. Set the jar out to ferment at room temperature. Leave it to ferment for 24 hours.
7. Once the kefir sour cream has fermented, it's time to remove the kefir grains from the cream.

Use a strainer and slowly pour the cream through the strainer. You might have to gently push the sour cream through the strainer while keeping an eye out for grains. As you find the grains, remove them from the strainer.

8. Store the kefir sour cream in an airtight container in the fridge.

Kefir Cultured Butter

The sour cream from the previous recipe can be used to make kefir cultured butter. This butter usually churns into a deep yellow color and is absolutely divine. Use it as spread or for other recipes that don't require cooking. After all the hard work spent churning this butter, you aren't going to want to cook it and kill the probiotic bacteria.

Ingredients:

1 quart kefir sour cream.
OPTIONAL: 1 teaspoon salt.

Directions:

1. Remove the kefir grains from the kefir sour cream.
2. Place the kefir sour cream into the fridge for a couple hours to slow down the probiotic cultures.
3. You can either use a stand mixer or a butter churn to make butter. If using the stand mixer, set it to the highest setting you can use without flinging butter everywhere. Once you see small butter balls starting to form, reduce the speed of the blender to allow the butter to stick together.
4. If using a butter churn, get to work and start cranking. You might want to enlist the help of nearby family members, as it can take upwards of 20 minutes to churn kefir sour cream into butter.

5. Regardless of the method used, you'll be left with buttermilk and butter. Pour off any standing buttermilk. The buttermilk can be saved and used in other recipes.

6. Wash the butter with filtered water to remove any buttermilk that's left in it. Squeeze as much of the buttermilk out of it as you can. It's important to be thorough in this step because buttermilk being left in the butter will cause it to go rancid at a much faster pace.

7. Add salt to the butter and stir it in if you want salted butter.

8. Store the butter in an airtight container in the fridge if you plan on using it quickly. Store it in the freezer for longer-term storage.

Sweet Kefir

If you're used to sweetened yogurt, plain milk kefir is probably going to be a bit too tart for your tastes. Adding a small amount of your favorite sweetener will bring it closer to what you're used to. Use an all-natural sweetener like raw honey or pure maple syrup and you'll be much better off than you would be eating the refined sugars and additives found in most commercial yogurts.

Ingredients:

1 cup milk kefir.
Pure maple syrup or raw honey, to taste.

Directions:

1. Add the maple syrup or raw honey to the kefir right before you plan on drinking it and stir it in. Don't add it and store the kefir in the fridge because the yeasts in the kefir will feed on the sugar.

Vanilla Kefir

When adding flavors to milk kefir, it's important to remove the kefir grains from the kefir before you add any additional ingredients. Adding ingredients to the kefir before the grains have been removed can do permanent damage to the grains. It may not destroy the grains, but it can change the way they perform.

Ingredients:

1 quart milk kefir.
1 tablespoon vanilla extract.
OPTIONAL: Raw honey, to taste.

Directions:

1. Start with fresh milk kefir. Make sure the grains have been removed.
2. Add the vanilla extract and stir it into the kefir. Alternatively, you can add whole vanilla beans to the kefir.
3. If you want vanilla kefir with little to no carbonation, place the kefir into an airtight container and transfer it to the fridge. The recipe is complete if you're using vanilla extract. If you added vanilla beans, let it sit for a day or two to give the beans a chance to infuse their flavor into the kefir.
4. If you want fizzy vanilla kefir, you need to do a second ferment after stirring the vanilla into the

kefir. Place the kefir into a jar and place an airtight lid on the jar.

5. Set the kefir out to ferment for 12 to 24 hours.

6. Once the kefir is carbonated to your preference, transfer the jar to the fridge. Open the lid to off-gas the container before moving it to cold storage.

7. If you like your kefir sweet, stir a tablespoon or two of raw honey into the kefir right before you drink it.

Vanilla Kefir Milkshake

One of my biggest weaknesses in life is a good vanilla milkshake. I can't resist them and would probably be ten pounds lighter if it wasn't for this one vice. This recipe isn't exactly like a vanilla milkshake, but it's close enough to where I can drink it and stave off the cravings. Most of the time.

The vanilla kefir from the previous recipe is used to make this recipe. I normally use plain vanilla kefir made with a single ferment, but if you want to try something different do a second ferment with the vanilla in the fermenting jar. A milkshake made with fizzy vanilla kefir will be carbonated and will taste similar to a vanilla cream soda.

Ingredients:

4 cups vanilla milk kefir.
¼ cup coconut cream.
1 ½ teaspoons ground cinnamon.
½ teaspoon stevia.
10 ice cubes.

Directions:

1. Add all of the ingredients to a blender and blend until smooth. Add additional ice cubes to the blender and blend them into the milkshake until the proper consistency is achieved.

2. Taste the milkshake and add more stevia, if you want it to be sweeter. You can use raw honey or pure maple syrup instead of the stevia, if you'd like.

Vanilla Walnut Kefir

Vanilla walnut kefir makes a handful of small changes to the vanilla kefir recipe that make a world of difference. It uses whole vanilla beans, which gives the kefir a richer, more intense vanilla flavor. It also fills the kefir with thousands of tiny black specks, which for some reason pleases me to no end.

The addition of ground walnuts takes this recipe over the top. You've got to try it yourself to believe it. For an even bolder flavor, try tossing a handful of fresh cranberries into the blender when you're blending everything else together.

Ingredients:

1 quart milk kefir.
¾ cup walnuts.
¼ cup pure maple syrup.
1 vanilla bean.
A handful of ice.

Directions:

1. Grind the vanilla bean in a spice grinder.
2. Add all of the ingredients to a blender and blend until smooth.
3. Serve immediately.

Double Chocolate Milk Kefir

Double chocolate milk kefir doesn't just contain chocolate in the kefir. It's got shaved dark chocolate sprinkled on top as well. I supposed you could eliminate the shaved chocolate if you'd like, but where's the fun in that? This recipe is great for those days when you're craving chocolate, but don't want to destroy your diet.

Ingredients:

1 quart plain milk kefir.
½ cup cocoa powder.
2 bananas.
¼ cup raw honey.

Dark chocolate shavings, for serving.

Directions:

1. Combine all of the ingredients except for the chocolate shavings in a blender and blend until smooth.
2. Drink immediately or chill before drinking. Sprinkle chocolate shavings on top of the kefir in each cup before you serve it.

NOTE: This chocolate milk kefir can be heated gently, so you have warm chocolate milk kefir, but be careful not to get it too hot. Too much heat will kill the probiotic bacteria in the kefir.

Chocolate Peanut Butter Kefir

This recipe is similar to the last one, but adds protein in the form of peanut butter. Sadly, it also eliminates the chocolate shavings, but there's nothing stopping you from adding them if you really want them.

If you're sensitive to milk, you can either eliminate it altogether or swap it out for almond milk. The more milk you add, the more drinkable this kefir will be. In the summer, I like to dilute it until it's almost as thin as milk and serve it over ice.

Ingredients:

2 cups plain kefir.
2 cups milk.
1 frozen banana.
¼ cup cocoa powder.
3 tablespoons peanut butter.

Directions:

1. Add all of the ingredients to a blender and blend until smooth.
2. Check the flavor and add more cocoa powder and/or peanut butter until the kefir is flavored to your preference.

Chocolate Cherry Kefir

It can be tough to get kids to drink kefir. I make this recipe and mix it 50/50 with milk and my pickiest eater drinks it like there's no tomorrow. This recipe can be made with plain kefir, but is better when a second ferment is done with the cocoa powder and cherries in the kefir.

Either fresh or frozen cherries will work for this recipe. If using frozen cherries, thaw them before adding them to the kefir for the second ferment. If you're adding the cherries to plain kefir and aren't going to do a second ferment, they can be added and blended into the kefir when you serve it.

Ingredients:

1 quart plain kefir.
¼ cup cocoa powder.
½ cherries, pitted.
Raw honey, to taste.

Directions:

1. After the initial ferment, remove the kefir grains from the jar.
2. Add the cocoa powder and pitted cherries to the jar and seal the lid.
3. Ferment the kefir for an additional 12 to 24 hours.
4. When the kefir's ready, dump the contents of the jar into a blender and blend it all together.

5. Add raw honey (or pure maple syrup), to taste, and serve chilled.

Cinnamon Chocolate Spice Kefir

This is one of my personal favorite recipes. It would probably taste great heated up like hot chocolate, but I've always been too scared to do it because I'm worried about killing the probiotic cultures. I do know it tastes great when you add a couple tablespoons of it to lukewarm coffee. Luckily, it's still pretty good without being heated and can be poured over ice when you want something cold and refreshing.

Ingredients:

1 quart plain kefir.
1 cinnamon stick.
½ teaspoon nutmeg.
¼ cup cacao powder.
3 tablespoons raw honey.

Directions:

1. Remove the grains from the plain kefir immediately after the first ferment. Blend the nutmeg and cacoa powder into the kefir.
2. Add the cinnamon stick to the fermenting jar.
3. Place an airtight lid onto the fermenting jar and allow the kefir to ferment for an additional 12 hours.
4. Remove the cinnamon stick and discard it. Dump the contents of the jar into a blender and blend until smooth.

5. Store the kefir in the fridge until you're ready to serve it. This kefir is best served within a day or two.
6. Add raw honey, to taste, right before you serve the kefir.

Apple Cinnamon Kefir

Apple cinnamon kefir is good. So good, in fact, it's tough to only drink one cup without going back for seconds. As long as you don't use a lot of sweetener, going back for a second helping probably isn't going to do much harm, so feel free to have seconds.

Ingredients:

1 quart plain kefir.
1 tablespoon ground cinnamon.
2 apples, cored and peeled.
A pinch of nutmeg.
3 tablespoons raw honey.

Directions:

1. Combine all of the ingredients in a blender and blend until smooth.
2. Store in an airtight container in the fridge. Drink within a day or two for best results.

Probiotic Peanut Butter Banana Protein Kefir

If you work out and are looking for a way to add protein powder to your diet, you'll appreciate this recipe. It adds protein in the form of peanut butter and includes a scoop of your favorite protein powder for a double serving of protein in a single glass of kefir.

Ingredients:

2 cups plain kefir.
1 whole banana.
1 scoop of vanilla protein powder.
2 tablespoons raw honey.
2 tablespoons peanut butter.
1 teaspoon vanilla extract.

Directions:

1. Add all of the ingredients to a blender and blend until smooth.
2. Drink immediately for best results.

Spirulina Kefir Smoothie

I'm not going to lie to you and tell you I'm in love with the flavor of this smoothie. There's something about the aftertaste of spirulina I just don't care for. What I do like is the health value of spirulina, so I'm constantly looking for ways to add it to my diet. This is one of the better ways I've found.

Spirulina is a form of algae that constantly pops up on lists of the best superfoods. It's high in natural protein and is a favorite amongst vegans looking to add protein to their diet. It's packed full of vitamins and nutrients and is believed to boost the immune system.

Ingredients:

1 quart plain kefir.
2 tablespoons spirulina powder.
4 bananas.
3 cups blueberries.
3 tablespoons raw honey.
A handful or two of ice.

Directions:

1. Add all of the ingredients except for the ice to a blender and blend until smooth.
2. Add the ice and blend it in.
3. Serve immediately.

Blueberry Kefir

Blueberries are a great addition to milk kefir because they rank amongst the top fruits and vegetables when it comes to antioxidant capacity. They're packed full of a wide variety of phytonutrients that improve cardiovascular health, brain health and even the health of the retinas of your eyes (14).

When selecting fresh blueberries for kefir, choose blueberries that are in prime eating condition. They should be firm to the touch and have a deep blue color. Discard any blueberries with obvious damage or soft spots. Frozen blueberries can be used in this recipe, but should be thawed prior to blending them.

Ingredients:

1 quart plain or fizzy kefir.
1 to 2 cups blueberries.
Maple syrup or sucanat, to taste.

Directions:

1. Place the blueberries, kefir and sweetener into a blender and blend until smooth.
2. Store in airtight containers in the fridge.

NOTE: If you're making fizzy blueberry kefir, the blueberries can be added either before or after the second ferment. Adding them before the second ferment will result in some of the sugar in the blueberries being consumed during the fermentation process. I'd wait until after the second ferment to add the sweetener, so you can determine exactly how much needs to be added.

Peaches & Cream Kefir

This is hands-down one of the best tasting kefir recipes in the book. If you like peaches and cream, you're going to love this kefir. I tried it with both raw honey and maple syrup and maple syrup is the clear winner when it comes to flavor. The rich, deep flavor of the syrup melds perfectly with the tang of the kefir and the tart sweetness of the peaches.

Use peaches that are ripe, but not overripe. If they're starting to get soft spots, they're too ripe for this kefir. When selecting peaches for this recipe, choose peaches that are firm to the touch, but yield slightly to gentle pressure. Frozen peaches work well for this recipe. If you use frozen peaches straight out of the freezer, you'll end up with a peaches and cream smoothie.

Ingredients:

1 quart plain or fizzy milk kefir.
4 cups sliced peaches.
1 banana.
¼ cup pure maple syrup.

Directions:

1. Place all of the ingredients into a blender and blend until smooth.
2. Serve chilled.

Frothy Orange Kefir

If you like Orange Julius's, this beverage should be right up your alley. It's frothy and delicious and is a great drink to serve to both kids and adults on a hot afternoon.

Ingredients:

4 cups vanilla kefir.
1 cup milk.
1 can frozen orange juice.
¼ cup raw honey.
7 ice cubes.

Directions:

1. Add all of the ingredients to a blender and blend until smooth.
2. Serve immediately.

Fizzy Citrus Kefir

Instead of adding the citrus peel after the second ferment, this recipe adds the citrus peel to the kefir after the grains have been filtered out and leaves it in the kefir for the second ferment. This infuses a light citrus flavor into the kefir and makes for an interesting flavor meld.

I've tried orange, lemon and lime peels and they've all made good kefir.

Ingredients:

1 quart milk kefir.
Peels from your favorite citrus fruits.

Directions:

1. After the initial ferment, remove the grains from the kefir and transfer them to a different container of milk.
2. Add the citrus peels to the kefir you just removed the grains from.
3. Seal the container so it's airtight and leave it at room temperature for 12 to 24 hours. Start checking it once every couple hours after the 12th hour and transfer it to the fridge when it is carbonated to your preference.

Fizzy Raspberry Pomegranate Kefir

Raspberry pomegranate kefir is a recipe that's good when made with plain kefir, but elevates to great when it's made with fizzy kefir. You can try it both ways if you'd like, but I can almost guarantee you'll prefer it with fizzy kefir.

Ingredients:

1 quart fizzy kefir.
½ cup pomegranate seeds.
½ cup raspberries.
1 cup almond milk.
Raw honey, to taste.
10 ice cubes.

Directions:

1. Add the kefir, almond milk, pomegranate seeds and raspberries to a blender and blend until smooth.
2. Add honey, to taste, and blend it in.
3. Serve immediately.

Creamy Apricot Kefir

Creamy apricot kefir is equally good regardless of whether you use plain kefir or fizzy kefir. Using plain kefir makes it more like a milkshake, while using fizzy kefir makes it taste similar to an ice cream soda.

When choosing apricots for this recipe, select apricots that have ripened enough to where they've started to turn sweet. Slightly green apricots don't work well in this recipe, as it relies on the apricots for much of the sweetness. If you have to use apricots that aren't quite ripe, add extra honey to account for it.

Ingredients:

1 quart plain or fizzy kefir.
10 ripe apricots.
1 banana.
4 tablespoons raw honey.
1 teaspoon vanilla extract.
A handful of ice cubes.

Directions:

1. Add all of the ingredients to a blender and blend until smooth.
2. Serve immediately.

Persimmon Fruit Kefir

In passing, a persimmon resembles an heirloom tomato. I thought they were closely related to tomatoes for the longest time and passed them by when they hit store shelves during their local growing season. It wasn't until I tried one at a friend's house that I realized what I'd been missing out on.

Persimmons are sweet when allowed to properly ripen. If you bite into an immature persimmon, you'll be rewarded with a very astringent taste, so it's important to know how to identify ripe persimmons. Most persimmons darken to a deep orange color and their skin will be almost translucent when they're ready to eat. Others should be eaten before they reach this stage, so when in doubt, ask.

Ingredients:

1 quart milk kefir.
3 ripe persimmons.
1 tablespoon coconut oil, melted.

Directions:

1. Add the kefir and coconut oil to a blender.
2. Cut each of the persimmons in half and scoop out the flesh. Add the flesh to the blender.
3. Blend the kefir until smooth.
4. Serve immediately.

Pumpkin Pie Kefir

This recipe tastes quite a bit like drinking a piece of pumpkin pie straight from a cup. I usually make this recipe over the holidays when I have extra pumpkin and pumpkin spices left over from making pumpkin pies.

The graham cracker crumbs can be eliminated if you're on a gluten-free diet. They're just there to add to the illusion.

Ingredients:

1 quart plain kefir.
2 cups pureed pumpkin.
3 tablespoons pure maple syrup.
1 tablespoon pumpkin pie spice.
A couple handfuls of ice.

Graham cracker crumbs, for garnish.

Directions:

1. Add all of the ingredients to a blender and blend until smooth.
2. Taste the kefir and add more maple syrup, if necessary.
3. Serve immediately. Lightly dust the top of each glass with graham cracker crumbs when you serve the kefir.

Kefir Triple Berry Chocolate Smoothie

Notice the distinct lack of sweetener in this smoothie. It uses dates in lieu of the honey or maple syrup used in most smoothie recipes. Feel free to substitute in your favorite berries. Blueberries, strawberries, blackberries, raspberries and elderberries all can be used in this recipe.

This smoothie will be a bit on the thick side. Add more milk if you want a thinner smoothie. Coconut milk or almond milk both work well.

Ingredients:

3 cups milk kefir or fizzy kefir.
1 cup milk.
7 Medjool dates, pitted
½ cup blueberries.
½ cup strawberries.
½ cup blackberries.
2 tablespoons cocoa powder

Ingredients:

1. Combine all of the ingredients in a blender and blend until smooth.
2. Store in the fridge until you're ready to drink. This smoothie is best when consumed shortly after you make it.

Strawberry Kale Kefir

Everybody has heard of green smoothies. I introduce to you the "green kefir."

This recipe calls for kale, but there's no reason you can't substitute your other favorite greens into the recipe. I chose kale because it's packed full of vitamins, antioxidants and phytonutrients and is high in fiber to boot. A single serving of kale can give you more than 200% of your daily requirement for vitamin A and nearly 700% of the recommended vitamin K.

Ingredients:

2 cups plain kefir.
1 cup kale, chopped.
1 cup fresh strawberries.
1 cup ice.
½ teaspoon vanilla extract.
Raw honey, to taste.

Directions:

1. Add all of the ingredients to a blender and blend them together.
2. Drink immediately.

Cumin Mint Salted Lassi

Lassi is a refreshing traditional beverage native to India and Pakistan. It's a blend of yogurt, sugar, water and spices, with a bit of fruit occasionally thrown in here and there. I've substituted kefir for the yogurt in this recipe and have added cumin and mint. Feel free to eliminate the cumin and mint in lieu of your favorite spices.

The Indian black salt in this recipe is a salt known in India as *kala namak*. It can be purchased online or at grocery stores that cater to the Indian community. It's optional and can be left out if you don't like the way it tastes.

Ingredients:

1 quart fizzy milk kefir.
1 ½ cups milk.
1 cup mint leaves.
1 teaspoon ground cumin.
1 teaspoon salt.

Indian black salt, for serving.

Directions:

1. Add all of the ingredients except for the Indian black salt to a blender and blend until smooth.
2. Store this drink in an airtight container in the fridge until you're ready to consume it. Use it within a day or two of making it.

Avocado Ginger Mint Kefir

This smoothie that mixes flavors you wouldn't think would work together at first glance, but somehow manages to blend into a tasty beverage. If you have kids, they're probably going to dislike this smoothie, but the adults in the house may appreciate the way the buttery avocado melds with the ginger and mint.

The shaved dark chocolate is optional, but provides a nice contrast to the rest of the flavors in the smoothie.

Ingredients:

1 quart plain kefir.
2 avocadoes.
2 teaspoons ginger, finely chopped.
8 to 10 mint leaves.

OPTIONAL: Dark chocolate, shaved.

Directions:

1. Combine all of the ingredients in a blender and blend until smooth. Save a couple of the mint leaves for garnish.
2. Garnish each cup of kefir with a mint leaf and sprinkle a small amount of shaved dark chocolate on top when you serve it.

Honeydew Green Tea Iced Kefir

Call me old fashioned, but I think there's nothing better than spending a hot summer afternoon hanging out on the porch sipping chilled beverages while watching the kids hang out with their friends in the yard. It brings me back to the days when I used to do the same thing under the watchful eye of my parents as they sat and reminisced about doing the same thing when they were kids. Hopefully, my children will carry on the tradition, as it's a great way to unwind after a long day's work.

This recipe is a great choice when you want something light and refreshing. The fact that it calls for green tea is an added bonus, as I'm always looking for ways to add green tea to my diet.

Ingredients:

1 quart milk kefir.
2 cups strong green tea.
½ cup almond milk.
2 bananas.
1 honeydew melon.
2 tablespoons raw honey.

Ice cubes, for serving.

Directions:

1. Cut the honeydew melon in half and remove the seeds. Scoop out the flesh of the melon and add it to a blender.
2. Add the rest of the ingredients to the blender and blend until smooth.
3. Chill in the fridge until you're ready to serve it. Serve over ice.

Chia Kefir Pudding

Chia pudding is a dessert that's making the rounds on Internet as a healthy and delicious replacement for the sugar-filled desserts most people turn to after dinner. It uses all-natural ingredients and is only lightly-sweetened, but still manages to pass muster as a dessert. This version of chia pudding uses milk kefir to up the nutritional value even more.

The chia seeds puff up in the kefir and can be a little off-putting at first, but if you like tapioca, the puffy chia seeds aren't too far off in texture.

If you're lactose intolerant and can't handle regular milk, try almond milk or coconut milk. When I use coconut milk, I like to sprinkle shredded coconut on top for an added coconut boost. There's no reason to try and mask the coconut flavor…Might as well embrace it and bring it to the forefront.

Ingredients:

1 quart plain kefir.
2 cups milk.
¼ cup chia seeds.
3 tablespoons pure maple syrup or raw honey.
2 teaspoons vanilla extract.
1 ½ teaspoons coconut flour

Directions:

1. Add all of the ingredients to a bowl and whisk or blend them together.
2. Cover the bowl and place it in the fridge to chill for a couple hours.
3. Stir to recombine the milk and serve cold.

Kefir Oatmeal Pudding

Kefir oatmeal pudding takes a little planning ahead, as it has to be put in the fridge the night before you plan on eating it, but it's a great way to have a quick and healthy breakfast ready when you know you're going to be rushed in the morning. Try experimenting with different types of kefir and different blends of fruit and ingredients. The possibilities are endless.

Ingredients:

1 quart plain kefir.
1 cup oatmeal.
Sliced fruit (bananas, berries, peaches, mangoes, etc.).
Pure maple syrup, to taste.

Directions:

1. Add the kefir and the rest of the ingredients to a jar.
2. Place the lid on the jar and shake it up.
3. Add fresh fruit in the morning as topping and enjoy.

Kefir Banana Cocoa Pudding

Blend a couple avocadoes into kefir and add cocoa to it and you end up with a pretty good facsimile of chocolate pudding. My son figured out that if you put these in a popsicle mold, you end up with something similar to a fudgesicle.

Ingredients:

2 cups plain kefir.
2 avocadoes.
1 banana.
¼ cup cocoa powder.
¼ cup raw honey.
1 tablespoon vanilla extract.

Directions:

1. Add all of the ingredients to a blender and blend until smooth and creamy.
2. Taste the pudding and add additional honey, as needed.
3. Serve chilled.

Probiotic Eggnog

Eggnog is a traditional Holiday beverage that's usually made with milk. This recipe substitutes kefir for the milk to create probiotic eggnog. I'll leave it up to you whether you want to add rum or bourbon to it, but I will say this. Probiotic eggnog is every bit as good with a stiff shot of rum as regular eggnog is.

It may seem strange that only 2 cups of the kefir are heated with the eggs, but this is done for good reason. Heating the kefir kills off much of the probiotic bacteria. By reserving half of the kefir and adding it back into the eggnog after it's cooled, you're adding probiotic cultures back to the eggnog.

There is a lot of sugar used in this recipe, so drink it in moderation.

Ingredients:

1 quart plain kefir.
6 eggs.
½ cup sugar.
1 tablespoon vanilla extract.

Nutmeg, for garnish.
Cinnamon sticks, for garnish.

Directions:

1. Whisk the eggs until they're frothy.

2. Combine 2 cups of milk kefir, the eggs, the sugar and the vanilla in a saucepan over Medium heat. Cook for 15 minutes, stirring constantly.
3. Turn off the heat and wait for the contents of the saucepan to cool. Once cool, stir the rest of the kefir into the eggnog.
4. Place the eggnog into an airtight container and chill it in the fridge overnight.
5. Served chilled. Garnish by adding a cinnamon stick to each glass and sprinkling nutmeg on top.

Coconut Milk Kefir

Milk kefir grains can be used to ferment coconut milk, but the lactobacteria will start to slow down after a few batches. Coconut milk doesn't provide the grains the same nourishment they get from animal's milk, so they'll eventually start to struggle. In order to keep your grains happy and healthy, return them to animal milk to recharge after every couple of batches of coconut milk kefir.

Homemade or canned coconut milk works well for coconut milk kefir. Steer clear of the boxed milks and the milks that come in cartons that have added sweeteners and other additives. These additives can damage your grains if you aren't careful.

The first batch of coconut milk you ferment with your milk kefir grains may shock your grains and the ferment may be weak. If this happens, try another ferment. The second ferment is usually better.

Ingredients:

1 quart coconut milk.
2 to 3 tablespoons milk kefir grains.

Directions:

1. Wash your hands and the utensils.
2. Place the kefir grains into the fermenting jar.
3. Add the coconut milk to the jar.
4. Use a wooden or plastic spoon to stir the coconut milk and grains together.

5. Cover the jar with a thin towel or some cheesecloth and secure it in place.
6. Set the kefir to ferment at room temperature for 18 to 24 hours.
7. Check the kefir frequently after 12 hours have passed and move it to the fridge once it's thickened up to your preference.

Coconut Eggnog

If you don't drink dairy, you probably thought you were out of luck when it comes to eggnog. After all, dairy is one of the main ingredients in most eggnog recipes. Coconut eggnog uses coconut milk kefir instead of dairy to create a completely dairy-free eggnog.

Ingredients:

2 cups coconut milk kefir.
1 cup coconut cream.
1 cup coconut milk.
¼ cup pure maple syrup.
1 tablespoon vanilla extract.
1 teaspoon almond extract.

Whipped cream, for topping.
Ground nutmeg, for topping.
Coconut flakes, for topping.

Directions:

1. Add all of the ingredients to a blender and blend until smooth.
2. Place the eggnog into a jar and let it chill for an hour or two in the fridge.
3. Serve with whipped cream and either ground nutmeg or coconut flakes as topping.

Strawberry Banana Coconut Milk Kefir

Pretty much any berry or fruit can be blended into coconut milk to make a tasty smoothie. You can use either fresh strawberries or frozen strawberries. If you're using fresh strawberries and want your drink to be more like a smoothie, toss a handful of ice cubes into the blender with the rest of the ingredients.

Ingredients:

1 quart coconut milk kefir.
2 cups strawberries.
2 bananas.

Directions:

1. Add all of ingredients to a blender and blend until smooth.
2. Serve immediately.

Mango Avocado Coconut Milk Kefir

Mangoes and avocadoes are two ingredients most people would never consider mixing. I normally wouldn't either, but one day I decided to try this blend just for kicks and giggles and it was surprisingly good. It's not something I'd eat every day, but it is an interesting deviation from the norm.

Ingredients:

2 cups coconut kefir.
2 cups frozen mango chunks.
1 avocado.

Directions:

1. Combine the ingredients in a blender and blend until smooth.
2. Drink immediately.

Almond Milk Kefir

Almond milk is another non-dairy milk that can be used to make kefir. As is the case with coconut milk, you might have to make a batch of almond milk kefir and throw it out before the grains become accustomed to fermenting almond milk.

When used in almond milk, kefir grains typically need to be recharged in animal milk every few batches or they'll progressively get weaker and weaker. I have a friend who claims to have grains she can use over and over again in almond milk without swapping out the grains, so your mileage may vary.

Ingredients:

1 quart almond milk.
2 tablespoons milk kefir grains.

Directions:

1. Wash your hands and the utensils.
2. Place the kefir grains into the fermenting jar.
3. Pour the almond milk into the jar.
4. Use a wooden or plastic spoon to give the almond milk a quick stir.
5. Cover the jar with a thin towel or some cheesecloth and secure it in place.
6. Set the kefir to ferment at room temperature for 18 to 24 hours.

7. Check the kefir frequently after 12 hours have passed and move it to the fridge once it's thickened to your preference.

Almond Strawberry Kefir

Once you have almond milk kefir ready, this is a great way to use it. This beverage is the consistency of a smoothie and it's a great breakfast when you're on the run and need to throw something together real quick. The best part is you don't have to feel like you're cheating yourself out of a healthy breakfast because it's actually good for you.

You can use fresh strawberries for this recipe instead of the frozen strawberries it calls for. If you decide to use fresh strawberries, add an additional handful of ice to the blender.

Ingredients:

2 cups almond milk kefir.
2 cups frozen strawberries.
2 tablespoons almond butter.
1 tablespoon flaxseeds.
1 tablespoon chia seeds.
1 teaspoon vanilla.
2 tablespoons raw honey.
5 ice cubes.

Almond slices, for garnish.

Directions:

1. Add all of the ingredients to a blender and blend until smooth.

2. Garnish with sliced almonds and serve immediately.

Kefir Cheese

Don't limit yourself to just beverages when making kefir recipes. You can use kefir in most recipes that call for milk or yogurt. Kefir cheese is easy to make and can be used as a spread or you can use it in a wide variety of recipes that call for cream cheese.

Ingredients:

3 cups plain milk kefir.

Directions:

1. Place a stainless steel mesh strainer over a bowl.
2. Pour the kefir into the strainer. The whey will drip through the strainer into the bowl.
3. Cover the bowl and store it in the fridge overnight to allow the whey time to separate from the kefir.
4. The next morning, you'll have kefir cheese in the strainer and whey in the bowl.
5. Store both the cheese and the whey in airtight containers in the fridge until you're ready to use them.

The whey you have left over when you make kefir cheese is highly probiotic. It can be added to smoothies or you can use it to jumpstart vegetable ferments.

An alternative method of making kefir cheese requires that you place the kefir into a couple pieces of cheesecloth or a towel. Fold the cheesecloth up around the kefir to create a bag in which the kefir is held. Hang the bag so it sits over a bowl. The whey will drip through the cloth into the bowl. You can help it along by gently squeezing the cheesecloth.

Kefir Artichoke Dip

Kefir artichoke dip is a versatile dip recipe.

It's great dip to serve alongside artisanal breads when you're looking to impress people while hosting a party. It's also a great dip to snack on while watching the big game or when you want a healthy afternoon snack to hold you over until dinner. You can dip breads, chips, crackers and even vegetables into it and it can be used as a spread on deli meat sandwiches.

Ingredients:

1 cup kefir cheese.
½ cup parmesan cheese.
1 onion, chopped.
1 cup artichoke hearts, drained and finely chopped.
Sea salt and black pepper, to taste.

½ cup extra-virgin olive oil.
1 egg yolk.
3 tablespoons fresh lemon juice.
½ teaspoon mustard powder.

Directions:

1. Add 1 teaspoon of the olive oil to a skillet over Medium-High heat. Cook the onions until they turn translucent.

2. Add the egg yolk, lemon juice, mustard powder and the rest of the olive oil to a bowl and whisk them together.
3. Add the kefir cheese to the bowl and blend it in.
4. Add the rest of the ingredients to the bowl and mix well.
5. Place the bowl into the fridge and chill the artichoke dip for a couple hours before serving.

Kefir Onion Dip

Kefir onion dip is a great recipe to break out for the big game or for those days when you feel like snacking on some vegetables and dip. The best part about it is this dip is guilt-free. It's made with kefir cheese, so you're adding probiotics, vitamins and minerals to your diet instead of the chemicals and unhealthy vegetable oils found in commercial dips.

Ingredients:

2 ½ cups kefir cheese.
2 large onions, finely chopped.
2 garlic cloves, minced.
2 tablespoons fresh lemon juice.
1 teaspoon paprika.
A pinch of cayenne pepper.
Sea salt and black pepper, to taste.

1 tablespoon extra-virgin olive oil.
Sliced green onions, for garnish.

Directions:

1. Add the olive oil to a skillet over Medium-High heat. Chop the onions and add them to the skillet. Cook until the onions start to turn translucent. Turn off the heat and wait for the onions to cool.

2. Add the onions to a food processor or blender, along with the rest of the ingredients. Pulse until the ingredients are combined.
3. Place the onion dip into a bowl or jar. Cover the container and store it in the fridge for at least a couple hours.
4. Slice the green onions into thin slices and place on top of the onion dip as garnish before serving.

Probiotic Vegetable Dip

Put this vegetable dip out at a party and it's guaranteed to get raving reviews. Just don't tell the people you're feeding it to that it's full of bacteria without explaining probiotics to them. You'll get some strange looks, for sure!

Make sure the avocadoes you select for this recipe are ripe, but not overripe. They should be firm to the touch, but yield slightly when you gently squeeze them.

Serve this dip with cucumbers, carrots, celery and tomatoes.

Ingredients:

2 cups plain kefir.
½ cup milk cream.
2 avocadoes.
1 green onion, chopped.
2 tablespoons raw honey.
1 teaspoon apple cider vinegar.
1 teaspoon fresh lime juice.
½ teaspoon oregano.
½ teaspoon dill.
A pinch of cilantro.
Sea salt and black pepper, to taste.

Directions:

1. Add all of the ingredients to a blender or food processor and blend them together until they form a creamy dip.

2. Keep the dip chilled until right before you plan on serving it.

Probiotic Ranch Dressing

Probiotic ranch dressing is yet another healthy replacement for foods you eat that should be healthy, but probably aren't if you're buying the commercial version. MSG, artificial flavors and added sugar are just a sampling of the ingredients you'll find in commercial ranch dressing. Take a look at the label on a bottle of your favorite ranch dressing the next time you pick it up and see how many items there are in the ingredients list that you can't identify what they are or why they're in there.

Ingredients:

2 cups plain kefir.
3 tablespoons fresh chives, finely chopped.
2 tablespoons fresh dill, finely chopped.
2 garlic cloves, minced.
1 teaspoon Dijon mustard.
½ teaspoon sea salt.

Directions:

1. Add all of the ingredients to a blender or food processor and blend until smooth.
2. Serve chilled.

Chicken Salad w/ Kefir Dressing

Here's another novel use for milk kefir. It can be combined with oil and vinegar to make salad dressing that isn't just passable. It's pretty darn good! I serve this salad with bacon bits or a bit of crumbled bleu cheese sprinkled on top.

Ingredients:

½ cup plain kefir.
3 chicken breasts, boiled and shredded.
3 cups mixed baby greens.
¼ cup onion, chopped.
¼ cup toasted pecan halves.
2 tablespoons extra-virgin olive oil.
2 tablespoons balsamic vinegar.
Salt and black pepper, to taste.

Directions:

1. Combine the kefir, olive oil, vinegar, salt and pepper in a sealable bag and shake until blended.
2. Add the rest of the ingredients to the bag and shake until they're coated with the dressing.
3. Chill the salad in the fridge for up to an hour before serving.

Kefir Fruit Bowls

Kefir fruit bowls are a quick and easy way to spruce up pretty much any fruit you decide you want to eat. Plain kefir pairs nicely with most sweet fruits. I've made this recipe with the following fruits and it's been good every time:

- **Apples.**
- **Apricots.**
- **Mangoes.**
- **Nectarines.**
- **Oranges.**
- **Peaches.**
- **Pears.**

In order to make the fruit bowls, all you have to do is cut the fruit into bite-sized pieces and get rid of any pits/seeds that are in the fruit. Place the fruit into a bowl and add half a cup of kefir for every 2 cups of fruit you have and stir it in until the fruit is coated.

Depending on the type of fruit used in the bowl, I sometimes like to add other ingredients. Sliced toasted almonds, pecan halves, walnut halves and a light dusting of cinnamon are all good additions. The end result is a delicious bowl of fruit and kefir that tastes great and manages to be good for you at the same time.

Kefir Cream Popsicles

This recipe takes full advantage of the fact that the probiotic bacteria in milk kefir don't die when you put them in the freezer. These creamy frozen treats are so delicious the bacteria will barely have time to go dormant before they're being woken back up.

Don't use metal popsicle molds when freezing kefir. The metal can react to the kefir and cause problems. I use BPA-free silicon molds and they work great.

Ingredients:

4 cups plain milk kefir.
1 ½ cups fruit.
1 cup raw honey.

Directions:

1. Place the fruit, kefir and honey into a blender and pulse until smooth. The variety of fruit you use is up to you. You can use individual fruits or you can combine fruits to create interesting flavors. Mango and pineapple works well together. So do strawberries and bananas.
2. Pour the kefir/fruit blend into the popsicle molds and place the molds into the freezer.
3. Freeze overnight.
4. Remove the popsicles from the mold and store them in a freezer bag. If you're storing them for a long time, wrap each popsicle individually. In

my house, they don't last long enough to worry about freezer burn.

Kefir Ice Cream

Here's a great way to store kefir in the freezer for up to a month. Making kefir into ice cream in order to preserve your kefir in the freezer is a great way to put any excess kefir you have up. Fermentation grinds to a halt when kefir is frozen and the probiotic bacteria go into dormancy. They'll wake up again once they warm up, presumably when you eat the ice cream.

This is a basic recipe that makes standard vanilla ice cream. Feel free to spruce it up by adding your favorite fruits, cocoa powder or any of your other favorite ice cream ingredients. This recipe works best when whole milk is used to make the kefir for the recipe. You can also try culturing the heavy cream before using it in the recipe for an added probiotic boost. It's done in the same manner milk is cultured.

You're going to need an ice cream machine to make this recipe.

Ingredients:

4 cups whole milk kefir.
4 cups heavy cream.
¾ cup maple syrup.
4 egg yolks.
1 teaspoon vanilla extract.
¼ teaspoon sea salt.

Directions:

1. Place the ice cream canister into the freezer and freeze it per the manufacturer's instructions.
2. Once the canister is frozen, it's time to prepare the ice cream. Add all of the ingredients to a blender or food processor and blend until smooth.
3. Pour the contents of the blender into the ice cream maker canister and place it in the ice cream machine.
4. Follow the directions that came with the ice cream machine to make the kefir into ice cream. This usually entails running the machine for up to an hour.
5. Transfer the ice cream to airtight containers before storing it in the freezer.

Lime (or Other Citrus) Sherbet

I've always been a sucker for a good sherbet.

Sherbet made with kefir is good sherbet on multiple levels. It's good to eat, is relatively good for you (at least compared to the commercial ice creams) and is a good way to get rid of any sugar cravings you may be having. Keep in mind there is a decent amount of sugar in this sherbet. While it is natural sugar, it's a good idea to only consume it in small quantities when the need for something sweet arises.

Ingredients:

1 quart plain kefir.
1 quart fresh citrus juice (lemon, lime, grapefruit, etc.).
Sugar, to taste.

Directions:

1. Place the ice cream maker canister into the freezer and freeze it per manufacturer's instructions.
2. Pour the kefir into a bowl and whisk the citrus juice and sugar into it.
3. Pour the contents of the bowl into the ice cream maker canister and follow the manufacturer's instructions for making ice cream.

Kefir Frosting

I'm a little bit torn when it comes to this recipe since I'm usually all about healthy foods. This frosting uses a large amount of powdered sugar, so it isn't really good for you. It is, however, made with kefir and contains probiotics, so it's marginally better for you than regular frosting. If you're making something you're planning on frosting, this recipe is a better choice than your average homemade frosting and it's a far-cry better than prepackaged commercial frosting.

Ingredients:

¼ cup plain kefir.
½ cup butter, softened.
3 cups powdered sugar.
1 teaspoon vanilla extract.

Directions:

1. Add the kefir, butter and vanilla to a bowl and whip until smooth.
2. Add the powdered sugar a little bit at a time and blend it in until the desired consistency is reached.
3. Place the frosting into the fridge for 30 minutes to allow time for it to thicken before using it to frost whatever it is you're planning on frosting.

Storing Your Grains

Making milk kefir is a fun and rewarding experience, but there may come a time in your life when you either don't have time to continue making daily batches of kefir or you decide you want to take a break. The good news is you don't have to toss out your grains and start over again the next time you decide to make milk kefir. There are a handful of methods you can use to store your grains for safekeeping until you're ready to use them again.

These methods are also a good way to store any extra grains you have that have grown in your kefir batches. It's a good idea to always have a set or two of back-up grains on hand just in case something happens to the set you're using. Batches of kefir occasionally go bad (or you forget about them in the cabinet) and you don't want to ruin your only set of grains. If you have a back-up set of grains stored away, you'll be able to continue making kefir regardless of what happens.

If you're looking to take a short break from making kefir, your best option is to place the grains into a container of fresh milk, seal the container and place the container into the fridge. Placing the kefir grains into cold storage will slow the fermentation process and the milk they're in will last 3 to 4 weeks before it needs to be changed. Once the grains have used up the lactose in the milk, they'll begin to starve. You may be able to bring them back if they've been left in the fridge for a longer period of time, but it's not going to be easy.

If you're planning on storing the kefir grains for more than a few weeks, they're going to need to be dried. Rinse the grains off with filtered water or spring water and set them out to dry at room temperature. Cover the grains with a paper towel as they dry to protect them from dust. It can take up to 5 days for the larger grains to dry. Alternatively, if you have a dehydrator available, the grains can be rinsed and dried at the lowest heat setting. Once the grains are hard and yellow, they're done drying. Store them in an airtight container in the fridge or even the freezer and they'll last up to 6 months.

One thing to remember when drying milk kefir grains is you're going to lose some of the grains during the process. When you rehydrate the grains, you'll be lucky if you get 75% of the grains to come back to life. I've heard people say they've only had a 50% revival rate, so it's best to put away twice as many grains as you think you're going to need just to be safe.

When the time comes to rehydrate the grains, follow the same directions you would when recharging newly purchased grains. Place them in a cup or two of milk overnight and switch the milk out daily until they revitalize. If they were in cold storage for a long time, it can take up to a month for them to rehydrate and start producing good milk kefir.

Frequently Asked Questions

Making milk kefir is far from an exact science, so you're likely to have questions. This chapter seeks to answer some of the more common questions that arise in the kefir community. If you're new to kefir, you're definitely going to want to read this chapter. Even if you aren't new, you might want to read it as a refresher.

Can I Grow Kefir Grains Myself?

That depends. If you're making milk kefir using kefir grains, your grains will more than likely grow and you'll produce a number of new grains in the process. If you're making kefir from a culture packet, you aren't going to be able to grow new grains. Likewise, kefir grains can't be grown by attempting to ferment milk with no kefir grains in it.

Why Aren't My Grains Growing?

There is the occasional batch of milk kefir grains that refuses to grow. As long as your grains are properly fermenting milk into kefir, this isn't a problem unless you want more grains. If this is the case, you may have to purchase new grains in order to try and get a batch that's willing to grow. First, make sure your current grains are being fermented under optimal conditions. Damaged or weak grains may stop growing until they've been allowed time to revitalize.

Is It Better to Buy Dried or Fresh Grains?

If you're planning on making milk kefir right away and live close to where the grains are shipping out of, live grains are a good option. On the other hand, if you aren't sure when you're going to start or you expect long shipping delays, dried grains will be the better option. Either way, you'll be able to make good kefir. You'll just have to rehydrate the dried grains first.

Can I Ferment My Favorite Milk with Milk Kefir Grains?

Most animal milks can be fermented with milk kefir grains. Non-dairy milks can usually be fermented as well. The following milks have all successfully been fermented using milk kefir grains:

- **Goat.**
- **Sheep.**
- **Cow.**
- **Buffalo.**
- **Camel.**
- **Human.**
- **Coconut.**
- **Almond.**
- **Soy.**
- **Rice.**

If fermenting non-animal milk, make sure you return your grains to regular milk after every few batches.

What Type of Milk Is Best for Kefir Grains?

That depends on the type of milk they're accustomed to. Full-fat animal milk is generally regarded as the best type of milk for kefir grains, but they can be used to ferment low- or even non-fat milks.

What About Raw Milk?

Yes, raw milk can be used to make milk kefir. Make sure you're getting your raw milk from a safe source and follow proper safety protocol when handling and consuming raw milk products.

Can Kefir Help With a Candida Infection?

Some people who suffer from *Candida overgrowth*, also known as a *yeast infection*, claim to have benefitted from consuming kefir. Candida albicans, the yeast responsible for yeast infections, is not one of the many yeasts found in kefir. The yeasts and bacteria in kefir may help the body crowd out Candida albicans and help bring the body back into alignment.

I'm Lactose Intolerant. Can I Drink Milk Kefir?

Maybe. Much of the lactose in milk kefir has been consumed by the bacteria and yeasts in the grains, so those who are mildly intolerant to lactose may be able to handle milk kefir. Longer ferments will eliminate more of the lactose from the milk.

How Much Alcohol Does Milk Kefir Contain?

After a short ferment, milk kefir usually contains less than 1% alcohol. Longer ferments in airtight containers can result in alcohol content of up to 3%.

Can I Eat the Grains?

Yes, kefir grains can be consumed. They don't taste great on their own, but some people like to add them to smoothies or other dishes into which they can be blended. Remember, a small amount of grains goes a long way. They're packed full of probiotics, so take that into consideration when adding them to recipes.

Why Are Some of My Grains Floating?

Carbon dioxide bubbles float through kefir during a ferment and can attach themselves to kefir grains. If enough of these bubbles stick to a grain, it can become buoyant and may float to the top of the fermenting jar. Older grains that have been neglected may also float to the top. If you've got a lot of floaters, it's important to assess the health of your grains to make sure they're getting enough dairy milk as food.

Is It Normal For My Grains to Stretch Out?

When the weather turns hot or the grains become stressed out, they can stretch out into ribbons. Once the stressors are eliminated, the grains should return to their normal shape and size.

Why Are All of My Ferments Different?

No two batches of kefir are going to be the same. Kefir grains are a living, breathing organism and are a product of their environment. Your batches of kefir will change based on environmental factors and you may notice differences from batch to batch even when nothing noticeable has changed in the fermenting environment. It's best to just roll with the punches and accept kefir for the dynamic creature it is.

Can I Break Larger Grains Up?

Yes, breaking larger grains up won't hurt them and is a good idea in order to ensure more of your grain is exposed to the milk it's trying to ferment. You can tear them apart with your fingers or use scissors or a knife to cut them apart.

How Can I Tell If My Kefir Has Gone Bad?

It's rare, but the occasional batch of kefir may go bad. Use your senses and exercise good judgment when assessing kefir. If it looks, smells or tastes different from what you think it should, dump both the kefir and the grains and start over. Kefir that's gone bad may smell foul or have colors in it that it isn't supposed to have. Check your kefir closely before consuming it.

Additional Reading

Book 1 in this series is on Fermented Vegetables. It can be purchased at the following location:

http://www.amazon.com/Fermented-Foods-vol-
Vegetables-Preservation/dp/1499224834

Works Cited

1. **Dubinsky, Angelica.** Kefir: The history of the magical grains. *Lingua Lift.* [Online] Sept 2012. [Cited: 4 23, 2014.] http://russian.lingualift.com/blog/kefir-history-recipe/.

2. *Kefir improves the efficacy and tolerability of triple therapy in eradicating Helicobacter pylori.* **Bekar, O, Yilmaz, Y and Gulten, .** 4, s.l. : J Med Food, 2011, Vol. 14. doi: 10.1089/jmf.2010.0099.

3. *Antimicrobial activity of broth fermented with kefir grains.* **Silva, KR, et al., et al.** 2, s.l. : Appl Biochem Biotechnol, 2009, Vol. 152. doi: 10.1007/s12010-008-8303-3.

4. *Friendly Bacteria In Alcoholic Milkshake Could Fight Food Allergies.* **Industry, Society of Chemical.** s.l. : Science Daily, 10 16, 2006.

5. *Probiotic Properties of Lactobacillus Strains Isolated.* **Yongchen, Zheng, et al., et al.** 7, s.l. : PLosOne, Vol. 8. doi:10.1371/journal.pone.0069868.

6. *Effect of Administration of Fermented Milk Containing Whey Protein Concentrate to Rats and Healthy Men on Serum Lipids and Blood Pressure.* **Kawase, M, et al., et al.** s.l. : Takanashi Milk Products, 1999.

7. *Kefir improves lactose digestion and tolerance in adults with lactose maldigestion.* **Hertzler, SR and Clancy, SM.** 5, s.l. : J Am Diet Assoc, 2003, Vol. 103, pp. 582-7.

8. *Antitumor activity of milk kefir and soy milk kefir in tumor-bearing mice.* **Liu, JR, et al., et al.** 2, s.l. : Nutr Cancer, 2002, Vol. 44, pp. 183-7.

9. *Apoptotic effect of a novel kefir product, PFT, on multidrug-resistant myeloid leukemia cells via a hole-piercing mechanism.* **Ghoneum, M and Gimzewski, J.** 3, s.l. : Int J Oncol, 2014, Vol. 44, pp. 830-7.

10. **Unknown.** Microbiome: Your Body Houses 10X More Bacteria Than Cells. *Discover Magazine.* [Online] [Cited: 4 12, 2014.] http://discovermagazine.com/galleries/zen-photo/m/microbiome.

11. —. The Link Between Homemade Kefir and Your Immune System. *Body Ecology.* [Online] 5 7, 2013. [Cited: 2 21, 2014.] http://bodyecology.com/articles/the-link-between-homemade-kefir-and-your-immune-system#.U1eQxvldUpk.

12. **Patterson, Michael-Paul.** Nutritional Value. *Ancient Health Wisdom Used In Modern Times.* [Online] 2007. [Cited: 3 12, 2014.] http://www.timelesshealth.net/kefir/nutritionalvalue2.html.

13. **Unknown.** FAQ: Kefir Grains 101. *Yemoos Nourishing Cultures.* [Online] [Cited: 4 1, 2014.] http://www.yemoos.com/faqmgrains101.html.

14. —. Blueberries. *The World's Healthiest Foods.* [Online] [Cited: 4 12, 2014.] http://www.whfoods.com/genpage.php?tname=foodspice&dbid=8.

CPSIA information can be obtained at www.ICGtesting.com
Printed in the USA
LVOW07s1222080116

469678LV00025B/926/P

9 781499 297171